LIVING THE DREAM

ACKNOWLEDGEMENTS

Dale Earnhardt Jr. 2004 "Living the Dream" was also a dream for Precision Publishing. When this project began, the goal was to take fans on a ride with this mega-star. In a short time, it became clear that there was no way to write such a story; the story and the driver grow by leaps and bounds each weekend. Whether it is a trip to victory lane or loading up early, the 2004 season has been a wild ride with new twist and turns along the way.

" Living the Dream" is not just a season review, in the pages that follow we have attempted to show the heart, desire, and talent of Dale Earnhardt Jr.

Dale Earnhardt Jr. is arguably one of the best drivers, if not the best in the world.
As we all know Junior had the best teacher possible, Dale Earnhardt Sr.
Junior has great sponsor support and a great crew, headed by crew chief Tony Eury Sr.
Each and every weekend Junior tightens the belts and thrills fans nationwide.
Most importantly, Junior is doing the thing he loves most, driving a race car, "Living the Dream".

The list of people that supported Precision Publishing is too long to list here,
but several deserve extra special thanks.
First, I want to thank Bill Seaborn for his insights and honest views.
I want to thank Fred Wagenhals at Action Performance, without Fred, this book may not ever have been published.
I want to thank Melissa Jones for helping proof and edit this book.
Thanks go to Greer Smith of the High Point Enterprise for taking on the writing responsibilities
and to all the photographers at CIA Stock Photography for finding just the right images,
and AP Worldwide Photos for supplying hard to find imagery.

I'd like to thank all the folks at DEI, especially Joe Hedrick and Kelley Earnhardt.

Lastly, heartfelt thanks to Dale Earnhardt Jr. for allowing this book to be published.

Please enjoy.

Design and layout by Host Communications, Lexington, Kentucky
Printing & Publishing Division
Executive Vice President - Craig Baroncelli
Creative Director - Richard Dark
Graphics Team - Duane Knight, Craig Watkins

NASCAR Publishing
Senior manager of Publishing - Jennifer White
Publishing Coordinator - Catherine McNeill

ISBN 0-9758854-0-5

CONTENTS

FOREWORD

Trudging through the infield of North Wilkesboro Speedway one fall day in the mid90s, I got my first glimpse of Dale Earnhardt Jr. as a stock-car driver. There was no indication that on the horizon loomed a winning NASCAR NEXTEL Cup series star who would be adored by millions. Dale Jr. came to the North Carolina track with his brother Kerry and his sister Kelley as all three sought to make the starting lineup for an annual Late Model Stock car race that routinely attracted drivers from throughout western North Carolina and Virginia. For this event, more than 80 contestants arrived seeking a place in a 36-car field as they wanted a chance to race on a track where the stars of the big league Cup circuit competed at that time. All three of the Earnhardts went home early when they failed to make the show that weekend. And so it was in the early days of Dale Jr.s' career, which started in 1992 when he and Kerry sold a go-cart for $500 and bought a Street Stock car for $200. In three years of racing Late Models from 1994-1996, Junior won just three races, leaving some observers to wonder if he had the ability to approach the success of his seven-time champion father and would he become the stock-car racing equivalent of Pete Rose Jr., never quite good enough to make to the major league of a sport where his dad was a star. A decision by Dale Sr. changed Junior's career. Needing a driver for his NASCAR Busch team in 1998, Dale gave Junior a try at the urging of his longtime crew chief Tony Eury Sr., who said "You've been spending your money on other people's children, why don't you spend it on your own." Junior then gave a glimpse of things to come and answered any doubts about his ability to make it beyond the Saturday night short tracks. Improving on Steve Park's three wins and rookie of the year award in 1997, Dale Jr. won a total of 13 races and NASCAR Busch Series championships in 1998 and 1999, earning invitations to compete in the International Race of Champions series. Combined with his grandfather Ralph's Sportsman championship in 1956 and his father's seven cup titles, Junior made his family the first to win NASCAR national championships in three generations. With the success in the Busch Series, Dale Sr. decided to move his son to the big time as the featured driver for Dale Earnhardt Inc. Junior made his debut in the 1999 Coca-Cola 600 at Charlotte and even then attracted a crowd. He participated in five races that year to get his feet wet and prepare for a rookie of the year bid in 2001. He eventually lost the rookie of the year title to Matt Kenseth, but certainly made a splash doing it. He picked-up his first win in March at Texas Motor Speedway, added a second win at Richmond in May and came back the following week to become the first rookie winner of the NASCAR all-start race at Lowe's Motor Speedway. That spine-tingling win still ranks as the most important on Junior's list and left his father beaming with pride as they stood in Victory Lane. His popularity sky-rocketed, fueled by an image crafted to appeal to the MTV generation as he wore his caps backward and emphasized a love for rock and roll and having a good time with his friends. He earned attention well outside the normal bounds of motorsports. He was included in *People* magazine's "most sexy men" issue in 2000, named one of *People's* "most intriguing people" in 2001, and one of its "50 most eligible bachelors" in 2002. He was the subject of two *Rolling Stone* pieces and the subject of a *Playboy* magazine interview. Also along the way, Junior has been the subject of episodes on the MTV series "Cribs" and "True Life." He was the focus of the VH-1 show "NASCAR Fever" and was featuredt in an episode of VH-1's "Driven." He's appeared on several of the network talk shows (Leno, Letterman, Today, Regis and Kelly and Jimmy Kimmel) and had roles in two music videos. His popularity continued to mushroom and in 2003 the depth of it verified when his fans voted him NASCAR's most popular driver a landslide win. He received 1.3 million votes, more than the rest of the top-10 drivers combined. While he was busy off the track, Junior also added to his legacy on the track. He proved the wins in 2001 were no fluke, coming back to triumph three times in 2001, and twice in both 2002 and 2003. Entering the 2004 season, he had nine victories and proved he was a "chip off the old block" on the superspeedways by winning four straight races at Talladega Superspeedway, where his father won a record 10 times. He pledged near the end of the 2003 season, in which he finished third in points, that his team led by Tony Eury Sr., was capable of winning the 2004 title. He did not disappoint as drivers battled for the title under NASCAR's new "Chase for the NASCAR NEXTEL Cup" format, in which the top 10 drivers at the end of 26 races vied for the crown over the final 10 events. From his victory in the season-opening Daytona 500 to the final race at Homestead-Miami Speedway, Junior remained in contention throughout. As in any campaign, it was filled with plenty of highs and lows. Here in pictures are snapshots of Junior's road to becoming a title contender plus his "ups and downs" in the "Chase for the NASCAR NEXTEL Cup."

DALE SR.
&
DALE JR.

Dale Jr. attempts to pass
Dale Sr. (blue car) on the inside
in an IROC race at the
Michigan International Speedway.

The moments just before the start of a race are some of the most intense for drivers. Dale Jr., gets last minute advice as he and Dale Sr. try to stay loose before the green flag drops.

Dale Sr. beams as a proud father and car owner while he poses with Junior in victory lane following the 2000 running of The Winston at Lowe's Motor Speedway. Junior became the first rookie to win the all-star race that features winners in a NASCAR series.

Dale Sr., usually reserved in public, lets his excitement show as he hugs Junior in victory lane while Junior climbs from his car after winning The Winston in 2000.

As a rookie, Dale Jr. received vital advice from his father as he learned the best way to get around the tracks on the NASCAR circuit. Here he gets some pointers as they watch practice for the Pop Secret 400 at North Carolina Speedway from the top of Dale Sr.'s transporter.

Father and son side-by-side at Daytona.

Triple-threat. Dale Earnhardt Sr. poses with sons Dale Jr. (l) and Kerry on pit road prior to the 2000 Pepsi 400 presented by Meijer at Michigan International Speedway. It was the only time all three competed in the same NASCAR race. Dale Sr. finished sixth. The day wasn't as kind to Dale Jr. and Kerry. Dale Jr. finished 31st, and Kerry was 43rd in a Chevrolet owned by Dale Sr.'s longtime friend Dave Marcis.

Dale Sr. and Junior share a moment before the beginning of a NASCAR Busch series race.

Dale Jr. rounds one of Martinsville Speedway's tight turns as his father eases ahead in the NAPA AutoCare 500. Dale Sr. clearly came out the winner between the two that day as he finished second to Tony Stewart. Dale Jr. was sidelined by a wreck on lap 406.

Dale Jr. focuses on getting down to business as he waits before the start of the Food City 500 at Bristol Motor Speedway. Although the lightning-fast half-mile has been kind to Junior during his career, it wasn't that day. Dale Jr. crashed on lap 402 and finished 38th, one spot ahead of his father.

NASCAR BUSCH SERIES

Dale Jr. smokes his tires doing a burnout at Miami-Homestead Speedway in celebration of his second straight Busch championship. Junior finished 280 points ahead of Jeff Green and had the title clinched going into the final race. He won six races (including three in a row at Dover, South Boston and Watkins Glen in June), three poles, led 23 events and took home $1,680,549.

Dale Jr. and crew pose with the 1999 championship trophy following the season finale at Miami-Homestead Speedway. As in 1998, Junior had the championship clinched going into the final race. But this time he finished the campaign in style, leading 98 laps and finishing second to race-winner Joe Nemechek.

Dale Jr. kisses the 1998 NASCAR Busch Series championship trophy following the final race of the year at Miami-Homestead Speedway. Junior had enough of a lead that he had the title clinched going into the 300-mile event, where he was sidelined by engine failure and finished a season-worst 42nd. Despite earning just 47 points, he had enough of a cushion to beat Matt Kenseth by 48 points for the championship. Junior won a total of five race, three poles and $1,332,701.

ABOVE.
Dale Jr. poses with the trophy after winning the 1998 Kroger 200 at Indianapolis Raceway Park by1.498 seconds over Elliott Sadler. It was his fourth victory of the season.

VICTORY LANE

Virtually all drivers now celebrate victories by doing burnouts. Dale Jr. is one of the best in that category and here he demonstrates his prowess by covering the Richmond International Raceway's front stretch in smoke as he spins the rear tires of the Budweiser Chevrolet after winning the Chevy American Revolution 400 in May 2004.

Dale Jr. lifts the trophy following a win in the 2003 Aaron's 499, his fourth straight victory at Talladega Superspeedway.

Dale Jr. puts an arm around the Golden Corral 500 trophy. It was his second win of 2004 and his first at Atlanta Motor Speedway.

IROC SERIES

In the only time they came to the checkered racing for the win, Dale Sr. edges ahead of Junior to win by a foot in a heart-stopping ending to the 1999 IROC race at Michigan International Speedway. Rusty Wallace is finishing third.

Junior follows his father in the draft as they work past Eddie Cheever in a 2000 race at Michgian.

Dale Jr. leads his father as they draft in 1999 at Daytona International Speedway.

Dale Jr. jokes with an IROC mechanic preparing for his first IROC start in 1999 at Daytona International Speedway.

Junior drives a battered car to the pits after crashing in the opening race of the 1999 IROC series at Daytona, his first IROC race ever.

PIT ROAD

Quick work of the pit crew can salvage good days out of potentially bad ones. Dale Jr.'s team beats out a crushed fender and front bumper in the 2003 GFS Marketplace 400 at Michigan International Speedway.

The DEI crew uses tape to make the bumper of the Budweiser Chevrolet more aerodynamic after it was crunched in an early crash in the 2003 Aaron's 499 at Talladega Superspeedway. Dale Jr. was not slowed by the damage and won the race.

The DEI team is caught in action halfway through a stop after changing right-side tires in the 2003 Pennsylvania 500 at Pocono. The front-tire carrier rolls the used tire toward the pit wall while the jackman and tire changer hustle to change left-side tires.

THE PIT CREW

Under the direction of Tony Eury Sr., the "Over-the-wall" crew for the No.8 team has been instrumental in Dale Jr.'s success in 2004. Quick pit stops, good fuel mileage and pit strategy repeatedly picked up positions to help solidify top finishes.

These are the men who were responsible for that success at the end of the season:

Tony Eury Sr.
Position: Crew chief
Hometown: Kannapolis, NC
Resides: Kannapolis, NC
Uncle of Dale Jr.
Known as Pops
Longtime friend of Dale Sr. began working on Dale Sr.'s Busch car part-time at night in 1982. Began working full time in 1986 for Dale Sr.'s Busch team which became DEI in 1988. Convinced Dale Sr. to give Dale Jr. a chance in Busch car in 1998, saying "You are wasting money on other people's kids. Why don't you waste it on your own?"

Tony Eury Jr.
Position: Car chief
Resides: Kannapolis, NC
Cousin of Dale Jr.
Years with DEI: 12
Involved with racing as long as "I can remember." Began working on race cars in the shop of his grandfather, noted car builder Robert Gee. Came to work with team with father Tony Eury Sr. to field Busch cars driven by Dale Earnhardt Sr.

Danny Earnhardt
Position: Front-tire carrier
Hometown: Kannapolis NC
Resides: Mooresville NC
Years with team: From before the start and before Dale Sr.'s youngest brother, known as "Uncle Danny" around the team
Works with Chance2 Busch team during week

Kevin Pennell
Position: Jackman
Hometown: Kannapolis, NC
Resides: Mooresville, NC
Joined DEI in 1995
Also is general mechanic

Phil Drye
Position: Front tire carrier
Hometown: Concord, NC
Resides: Concord, NC
Left the No. 17 Roush Racing team to join DEI in 2003

Troy Prince
Position: Rear tire carrier
Hometown: Yorke, ME
Resides: Davidson, NC
Left the No. 21 Wood Brothers team to join DEI in 2003

Greg Burkhardt
Position: Rear tire changer
Hometown: Sheridan, WY
Resides: Archdale, NC
Left the No. 10 MBV Motorsports team to join DEI in Aug. 2004

Jeff Clark
Position: Gasman
Hometown: Charlotte, NC
Resides: Charlotte, NC
Joined DEI in 1999
Owns motorcycle customizing business

Barry "B" Hoover
Position: Windshield cleaner and driver comfort
Hometown: Charlotte NC
Resides: Charlotte, NC
Joined DEI in 1998

Craig Lund
Position: Catch can man
Hometown: Edgerton, WI
Resides: Concord, NC
Joined DEI in 2002

SPEEDWEEKS

Dale Jr.'s crew pushes
the Budweiser Chevrolet
through the garage area
during a practice session.

Dale Jr. climbs from his car, pumping his arm in triumph, as his crew gathers to celebrate victory in stock car racing's most important race, the Daytona 500. The crowd gathered after Junior stopped on the front stretch to celebrate in view of the main grandstand.

The Budweiser Chevrolet sits in the foreground as Dale Jr. and his crew pose in the background following Dale Jr.'s victory in a Daytona 500 qualifying race. The Daytona 500 is the only race on the NASCAR NEXTEL Cup Series which uses qualifying races to determine its starting lineup. All of the other 35 races use qualifying laps.

DAYTONA 500

FEBRUARY 15, 2004
DAYTONA INTERNATIONAL SPEEDWAY

Still parked at the

start-finish line,

Dale Jr. is surrounded

by a crush of media

as he pumps a fist

while saluting fans.

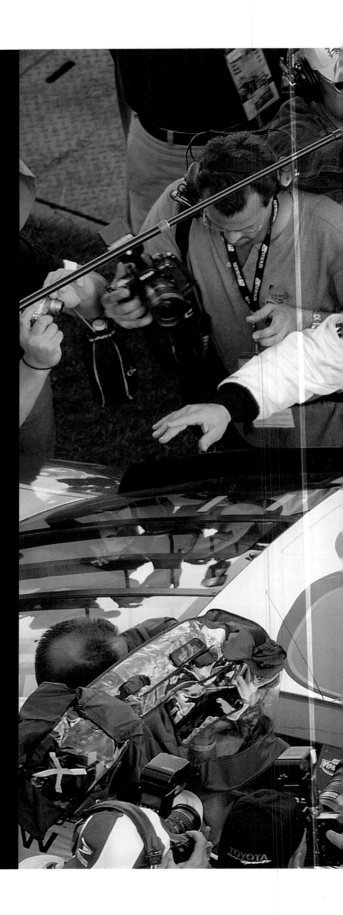

Stopping at the start-finish line, Dale Jr. raises his arms in jubilation as he climbs from his car to start the celebration in front of a packed front stretch grandstand.

Dale Jr. sprays champagne in victory lane while his crew retaliates by dousing him with Budweiser beer.

S U B W A Y
4 0 0

F E B R U A R Y   2 2 ,   2 0 0 4
N O R T H   C A R O L I N A   S P E E D W A Y

Dale Jr. leans beside

his car as the time

to climb behind

the wheel of

the Budweiser

Chevrolet approaches.

Dale Jr. speeds along the front stretch on the way to fifth place in the final NASCAR NEXTEL Cup Series race at North Carolina Motor Speedway. It was his only top five finish in seven starts at the 1.107-mile track.

Hurry up and wait. Junior stands beside the Budweiser Chevrolet while waiting for his turn to qualify.

UAW DAIMLER CHRYSLER 400

MARCH 7, 2004
LAS VEGAS MOTOR SPEEDWAY

Dale Jr. leads a pack
into the first turn at
Las Vegas Motor Speedway.
Following the closest
are Jeff Gordon (right)
and Joe Nemechek.

Dale Jr. and Tony Eury Jr. go over notes as they discuss chassis adjustments needed for the Budweiser Chevrolet.

Dale Jr. battles rookie sensation Kasey Kahne on the front stretch as Kurt Busch follows. Kahne finished second to Matt Kenseth. Busch was ninth and Junior thirty-fifth.

GOLDEN CORRAL 500

MARCH 14, 2004
ATLANTA MOTOR SPEEDWAY

Dale Jr. pulls away from
Jeremy Mayfield in the
waning laps of the
Golden Corral 500.
After the final round of
pit stops, Junior regained the
lead from Mayfield with
16 laps to go and sprinted
to a 4.5 second victory.

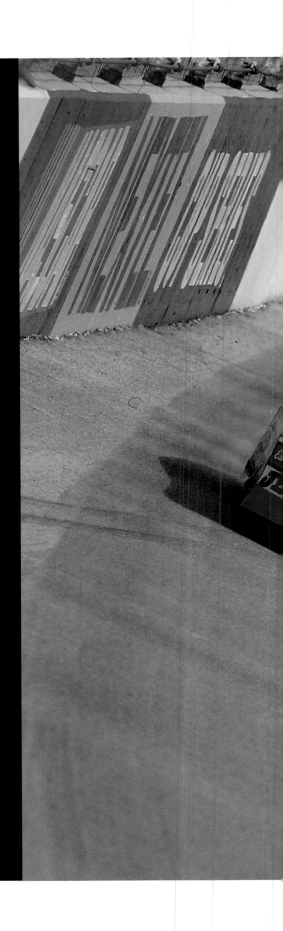

Sticking with the current tradition in NASCAR NEXTEL Cup Series racing, Dale Jr. smokes his tires doing a victory burnout after taking the checkered flag at Atlanta Motor Speedway.

Oh what a feeling! Dale Jr. lets out a laugh as he soaks up the thrill of winning for the first time at Atlanta Motor Speedway, where his father won nine times.

CAROLINA DODGE DEALERS 400

MARCH 21, 2004
DARLINGTON RACEWAY

Dale Jr. rockets down the
straightaway on the way to
leading 18 laps and
finishing 10th at the
"Track Too Tough to Tame."
He moved within 21 points
of Matt Kenseth,
who finished 31st.

Crewmen roll tires out of the way as Dale Jr. gets fresh rubber and fuel.

With helmet resting nearby on the top of his car, Dale Jr. awaits the start of practice at Darlington Raceway.

FOOD CITY
5 0 0

MARCH 28, 2004
BRISTOL MOTOR SPEEDWAY

A lot of people in a little space.
A sell-out crowd of 150,000, drawn by
unpredictable short-track action, packs the
Bristol's football stadium-like stands that
soar as much as six stories above
the .533-mile concrete bowl. Demand for
seats is so great that the track holds a
lottery to distribute available tickets.

Dale Jr. hugs the bottom groove in one of Bristol Motor Speedway's turns banked 36-degrees.

LEFT.
Holding a bottle of water, Dale Jr. cools off following a practice session. Although it was late March, drivers worked up a sweat because of the physical strain caused by the "g forces" created by racing on Bristol's steep banking.

RIGHT.
Looking visibly drained, Dale Jr. relaxes after the final practice session of the day at Bristol.

SAMSUNG RADIO SHACK 500

APRIL 4, 2004
TEXAS MOTOR SPEEDWAY

Dale Jr. spends a
quiet moment in
a corner of the
garage building, away
from the hustle and bustle
near the team's transporter.

One can of fuel goes in the Budweiser Chevrolet as another crewman holds a second during a pit stop at Texas Motor Speedway. Each can holds 11 gallons and two are needed to fill a 22-gallon fuel cell.

Dale Jr. rounds the turn with rookie Kasey Kahne in pursuit. Junior finished third and moved within 35 points of leader Matt Kenseth.

ADVANCED AUTO PARTS 500

APRIL 18, 2004
MARTINSVILLE SPEEDWAY

Dale Jr. rounds the turn ahead

of Kevin Harvick and Elliott Sadler.

Junior led 154 laps, finished

third and regained the lead

in NASCAR NEXTEL Cup Series

standings by five points over Kurt Busch.

The DEI crew hustles into action as Dale Jr. slides into his pit for service. The pit road at Martinsville is narrow and can be easily blocked, making quick pit stops crucial.

Dale Jr. stares intently
during a practice session
for the Advance Auto
Parts 500.

AARON'S 499

APRIL 25, 2004
TALLADEGA SUPERSPEEDWAY

The Budweiser Chevrolet goes through pre-race technical inspection. The inspection process at Talladega and Daytona is lengthy because of special rules that include installation of carburetor restrictor-plates, NASCAR provided springs and shocks, and spoiler regulations.

In a familiar position, Junior leads the draft through Talladega's tri-oval. Junior led a race-best 57 laps in the 188-lap event.

Dale Jr. stays beside Jeff Gordon as they follow the pace truck during a race-ending caution period that began with four laps to go. Dale Jr. and Gordon were racing for the lead when the yellow was waved. NASCAR ruled Gordon was in front when the running order was frozen when the caution period started, leaving Gordon the winner when there was no green flag restart. Fans littered the front stretch with beverage cans protesting the yellow-flag ending. With the second-place finish, Junior increased his points lead to 95 over Matt Kenseth.

Fans pack the stands as Dale Jr. leans against the car on the starting grid, getting ready to pursue another Talladega Superspeedway victory.

AUTO CLUB 500

MAY 2, 2004
CALIFORNIA SPEEDWAY

Dale Jr. leads

a line of cars past

Scott Wimmer (CAT)

on California

Speedway's front stretch.

Jackman Kevin Penell whips around the Budweiser Chevrolet as the crew begins to change left-side tires in a four-tire stop.

Dale Jr. stands beside the Budweiser Chevrolet as race time nears. He finished 19th, but kept the NASCAR NEXTEL Cup Series points lead by 25 over Matt Kenseth.

CHEVY AMERICAN REVOLUTION 400

MAY 15, 2004
RICHMOND INTERNATIONAL RACEWAY

The entire

DEI crew

poses in

victory lane

with the Chevy

400 trophy.

Plumes of tire smoke billow as Dale Jr. turns victory doughnuts at Richmond International Raceway's start-finish line.

LEFT.
Dale Jr. receives
congratulations from
race runner-up
Jimmie Johnson.

RIGHT.
Crew members pour beer
on Dale Jr., interrupting his
photo session beside the
Chevy 400 trophy. The win
was Dale Jr.'s second at
Richmond.

COCA COLA 600

A crewman rolls a tire out of the way as Dale Jr. gets service under the lights at the Lowe's Motor Speedway during the nighttime portion of the Coca-Cola 600. Dale Jr. finished sixth and left with a five-point lead over race winner Jimmie Johnson.

Dale Jr. zips around one of Lowe's Motor Speedway's banked asphalt turns. Handling is a key factor in the 600 because of the track's dramatic change going for the heat of the day to the coolness of the evening.

Sitting behind the wheel of a NASCAR NEXTEL Cup Series car is a very restrictive environment for safety reasons. Just how confining is shown in this picture of Dale Jr. tightly held in place by safety belts.

MBNA 400
"A SALUTE TO HEROES"
JUNE 6, 2004
DOVER INTERNATIONAL SPEEDWAY

Wrapping his arm around the steering wheel, Dale Jr. sits raring to take the green flag in the MBNA 400. The view of Dale Jr.'s helmet is partially blocked by a side guard that extends from the seat to prevent injures from a driver's head and neck from snapping to one side. Among other safety features visible are Junior's fire-resistant driving gloves, and in the background, a window net that helps keep a driver's head inside the car.

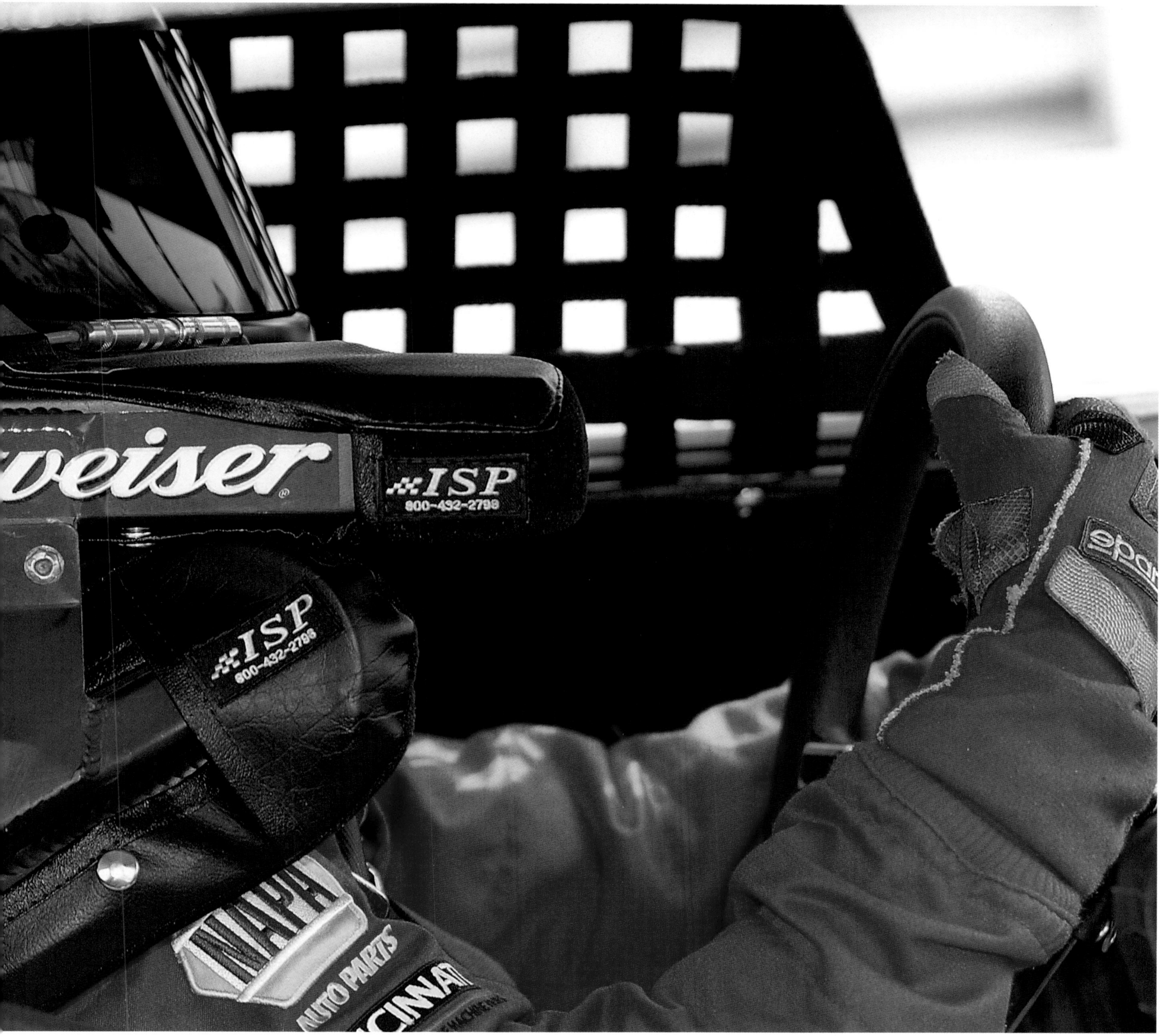
ISP
800-432-2798
ISP
800-432-2798
AUTO PARTS

Dale Jr. stands beside the Budweiser Chevrolet awaiting command to climb aboard and buckle up for 400 miles. Junior, a former Dover winner, started twenty-sixth. He finished third by dodging wrecks that took out a number of top contenders.

Dale Jr. scoots around one of the banked concrete turns at Dover International Speedway, one of three NASCAR NEXTEL Cup Series tracks with concrete pavement. The others are Bristol Motor Speedway and Martinsville Speedway.

P O C O N O
5 0 0

J U N E   1 3 ,   2 0 0 4
P O C O N O   R A C E W A Y

Known for his fun-loving

attitude, Junior is all

business as he

sternly looks across

the garage area

during practice.

Bud
Bud
Remington
Arms
Gillette
YOUNG GUNS
RITZ
CRACKERS
NASCAR
NEXTEL
CUP SERIES
DRAKKAR
NOIR
sparco

Dale Jr. rounds a Pocono Raceway turn to the outside of Jeff Burton.

Dale Jr. swings around Mark Martin. Junior finished sixth as his points lead over race winner Jimmie Johnson shrank to 58 points.

D H L 4 0 0

Dale Jr. battles DEI teammate Michael Waltrip for position. Waltrip finished tenth behind winner Ryan Newman. Junior struggled to twenty-first, just his third finish outside of the top 10 in the first 15 races of the season, and dropped seven points behind new points leader Jimmie Johnson.

As is the case at virtually all NASCAR NEXTEL Cup Series races, the stands were packed at Michigan International Speedway. Races at the two-mile track take on extra importance to the teams because it is the tour stop nearest the headquarters of General Motors and Ford in the Detroit area.

A fireman douses a flash fire that erupted when spilled fuel ignited during Dave Blaney's pit stop. Blaney finished 15th.

DODGE
SAVE MART
350

JUNE 27, 2004
INFINEON RACEWAY

Dale Jr. crests a hill at Infineon Raceway.

The road course poses a unique challenge with

its changes in elevation and twisting turns.

Dale Jr. makes his way through a series of S-curves known as the "esses." Junior finished ninth after leading nine laps on a day when he fell 27 points behind Jimmie Johnson.

Dale Jr. collects his thoughts and reflects as he prepares to slide into the Budweiser Chevrolet for the Save Mart 350.

PEPSI 400

A statue of Dale Earnhardt Sr.

greets patrons near

the entrance of

Daytona International Speedway,

where he won a record

34 times. The statue depicts

Earnhardt holding the trophy

in victory lane after winning

the 1998 Daytona 500.

Dale Jr. sets the pace in the Pepsi 400, followed by Greg Biffle (16), Brian Vickers (25), Jimmie Johnson (48) and eventual winner Jeff Gordon (24). Junior led a total of 23 laps in the 160-lap event.

Dale Jr. and teammate Michael Waltrip work together in the draft at Daytona International Speedway. Try as they might, they were unable to maneuver past the Hendrick Motorsports tandem of winner Jeff Gordon and runner-up Jimmie Johnson. Junior finished third and with a five point bonus for leading, stayed 27 points behind Johnson. Waltrip wound up 13th.

TROPICANA 400

JULY 11, 2004
CHICAGOLAND SPEEDWAY

Dale Jr.'s helmet,
with HANS device
attached, sits atop
the Budweiser Chevrolet
during a break in practice.

Junior shares a light-hearted moment with Elliott Sadler, one of his closest friends off the track.

Dale Jr. rumbles through a turn with Greg Biffle on his bumper. Collected in a crash that started when Tony Stewart turned Kasey Kahne into the front stretch wall, Junior rallied to finish 22nd. He remained second in points, dropping 105 behind Jimmie Johnson.

Dale Jr. tumbles out of a burning Corvette CR-5 at Infineon Raceway. The car burst into flames when it backed into a barrier during practice for an American LeMans Series sports car race. A rescue worker then leads Dale Jr. away after his escape from the burning Corvette.

FLARE UP!

SIEMENS 300

JULY 25, 2004
NEW HAMPSHIRE
INTERNATIONAL SPEEDWAY

Rookie stripe? The bumper of the Budweiser Chevrolet wore a rookie stripe at New Hampshire when Martin Truex Jr. relieved injured Dale Jr. in the practice and qualifying and most of the Siemans 300. It marked the first time Truex drove a NASCAR NEXTEL Cup car in competition.

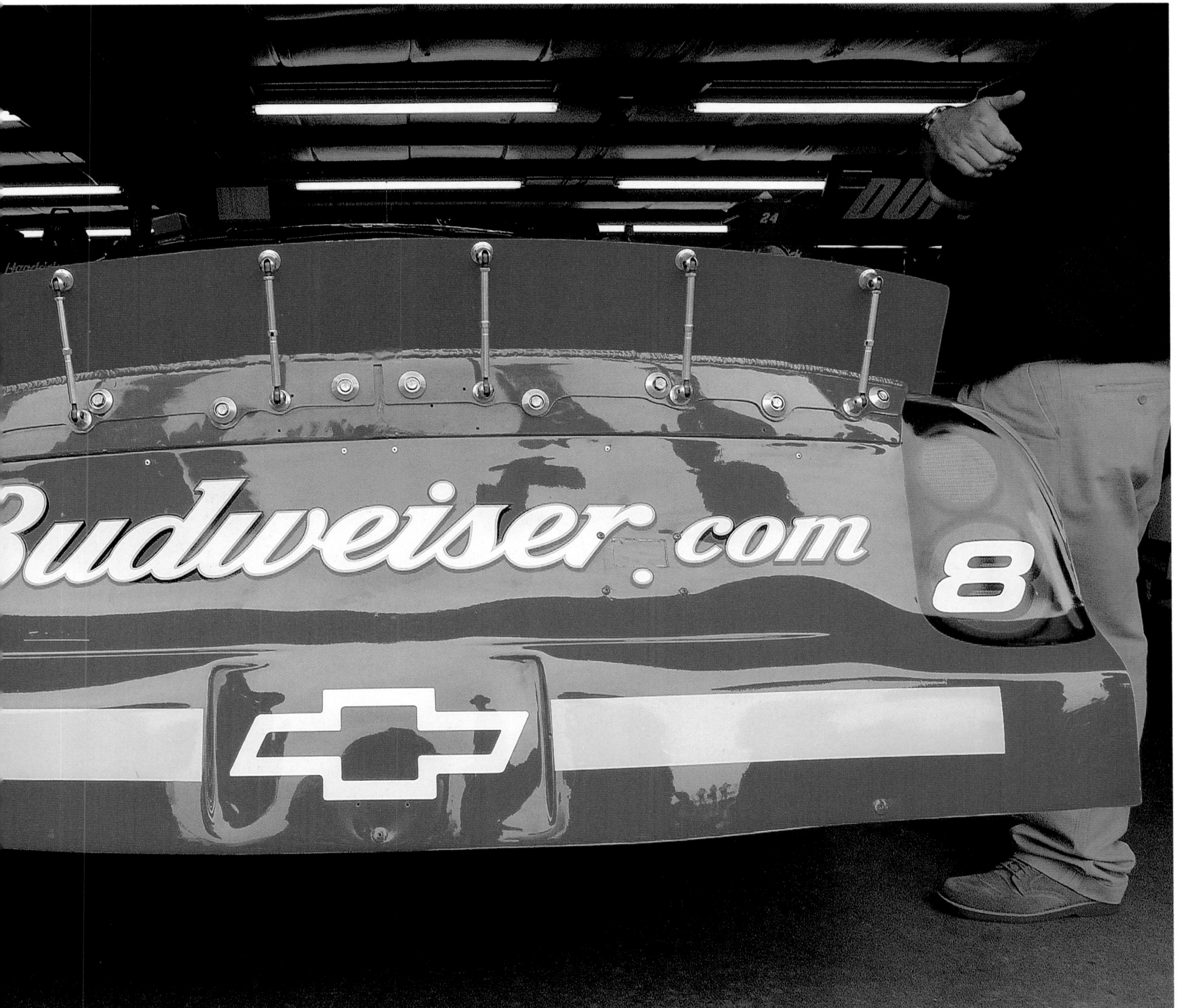
Budweiser.com
8

OPPOSITE PAGE.
Relief driver Martin Truex Jr. (RIGHT) backs into the first turn wall at the New Hampshire International Speedway after colliding with Ken Schrader on lap 142 of the 300-lap race. Hurting from burns suffered in a sports car crash a week earlier, Dale Jr. got out of the Budweiser Chevrolet after 61 laps and let Truex go the rest of the distance. They combined for a 31st-place finish.

PENNSYLVANIA 500

RIGHT.

With a burn area visible, Dale Jr. conserves his energy by sitting in the garage area during practice for the Pennsylvania 500.

FAR RIGHT.

Dale Jr. relaxes before the start of the Pennsylvania 500.

A crewman pulls Dale Jr. after only 53 laps in the Pennsylvania 500. Already a lap down, Earnhardt opted to get out during the first caution period and let John Andretti drive the Budweiser Chevy for the rest of the 200-lap race. They combined for 25th place as Junior dropped 267 points behind leader Jimmie Johnson, the race winner.

Still walking with a limp because of burns on his legs, Dale Jr. makes his way past an honor guard during pre-race ceremonies.

BRICKYARD 400

AUGUST 8, 2004
INDIANAPOLIS MOTOR SPEEDWAY

Dale Jr. leads Tony Stewart and Dale Jarrett around one of Indianapolis Motor Speedway's modestly-banked turns. Going without a relief driver for the first time since suffering burns three weeks earlier, Junior was on the verge of a top-10 finish when he was caught in a crash in the final lap and dropped 21 spots to finish 27th. Despite the misfortune, Junior gained points on leader Jimmie Johnson, who was sidelined by engine failure.

NASCAR officials and track workers replace a bale of foam slabs that make up part of the impact absorbing material in the speedway's SAFER barrier.

Dale Jr. looks at the packed stands at Indianapolis Motor Speedway before the start of the Brickyard 400.

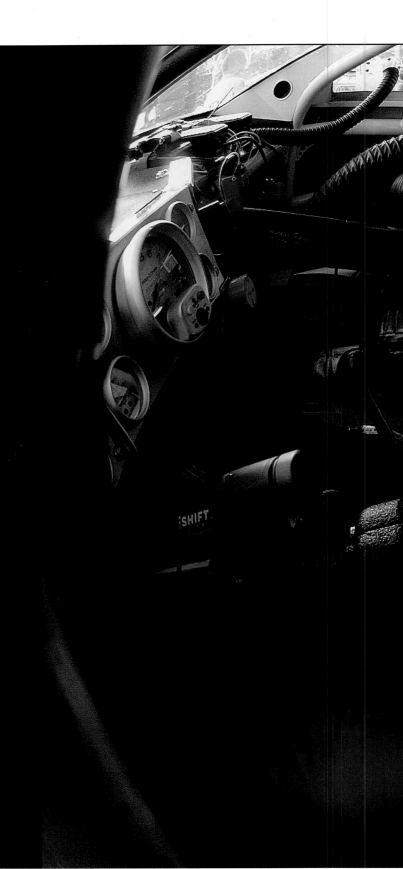

SIRIUS AT THE GLEN

AUGUST 15, 2004
WATKINS GLEN INTERNATIONAL

Dale Jr. is buckled in with helmet in place, gripping the steering wheel and ready to take to the track for the start of the Sirius at The Glen.

Dale Jr. rests his head on his hand during a break in practice.

Dale Jr. swings around one of The Glen's right-hand turns as Kevin Harvick follows. Dale Jr. finished fifth, as points leader Jimmie Johnson was sidelined by engine failure. Johnson, who finished 40th, left 128 ahead of Junior.

GFS MARKETPLACE 400

AUGUST 22, 2004
MICHIGAN INTERNATIONAL SPEEDWAY

Crewmen check under the rear of the Budweiser Chevrolet during a pit stop at Michigan International Speedway. Dale Jr. finished 21st and remained third in points as Jeff Gordon replaced Jimmie Johnson as the leader. Gordon finished seventh and Johnson was sidelined by engine failure.

SHARPIE 500

AUGUST 28, 2004
BRISTOL MOTOR SPEEDWAY

A set of four tires
sits stacked like dominoes
as cars sit parked on
pit road before practice.

ABOVE.
Dale Jr. laps Kenny Wallace on the way to his fourth victory of the year. Dale Jr. led the last 85 laps of the Sharpie 500.

LEFT.
Dale Jr. adds his name to the signature of winners in Bristol Motor Speedway's victory lane. The win moved Junior within 75 points of leader Jeff Gordon.

BELOW.
Dale Jr. puts the nose of the Budweiser Chevrolet against the front stretch wall, smoking his tires celebrating his first Bristol Motor Speedway victory.

POP SECRET 500

SEPTEMBER 5, 2004
CALIFORNIA SPEEDWAY

Mountains provide an
impressive backdrop
as fans jam the
California Speedway infield.

CHEVY ROCK AND ROLL 400

SEPTEMBER 11, 2004
RICHMOND INTERNATIONAL RACEWAY

Not a headache. Dale Jr. puts his hands on head while thinking about chassis setup on the Budweiser Chevrolet. He made the right decision and finished second in the Chevy Rock and Roll 400.

Budweiser
sparco
YOUNG GUNS
RITZ
CRACKERS
CHAMPION
The OUTLAW
Snap-on

Dale Jr. (left, back row) poses with the other nine drivers who qualified for the Chase for the NASCAR NEXTEL Cup. Left to right on the front row are Jeff Gordon, Jimmie Johnson, Jeremy Mayfield and Ryan Newman. On the back row with Junior are Matt Kenseth, Tony Stewart, Elliott Sadler, Kurt Busch and Mark Martin.

Dale Jr. goes to the inside as he races three-abreast with Matt Kenseth (17) and Mike Wallace.

SYLVANIA 300

SEPTEMBER 19, 2004
NEW HAMPSHIRE INTERNATIONAL SPEEDWAY

Junior blasts through the turn followed by Jeff Burton (AOL) and New England favorite Ricky Craven in his final race in the Tide Chevrolet. Burton finished 15th and Craven 17th.

Junior leads Matt Kenseth and eventual race winner Kurt Busch through a turn. When the checkered flag waved, Kenseth was second and Dale Jr. third.

Junior is second from left on the back row as the ten drivers in the Chase for the Championship pose with the NASCAR NEXTEL Cup Series trophy held by Jeff Gordon and Jimmie Johnson. Renowned jeweler Tiffany and Company crafted the 27-pound trophy from sterling silver. Along with Dale Jr. on the back row (from left) are Matt Kenseth, Jeff Gordon, Jimmie Johnson, Tony Stewart and Elliott Sadler. On the front row (from left) are Jeremy Mayfield, Kurt Busch, Mark Martin and Ryan Newman.

MBNA AMERICA 400

SEPTEMBER 26, 2004
DOVER INTERNATIONAL SPEEDWAY

Junior and Dale Earnhardt Inc. teammate Michael Waltrip fight for position on the Dover backstretch as Mark Martin follows. Junior finished ninth while Michael took 16th.

Dale Jr. buckles his helmet while talking to Martin Truex, Jr. as he prepares to get behind the wheel of the Budweiser Chevrolet for his qualifying run. Junior qualified 16th.

Dale Jr. listens as he spends a minute with friend and Chase for the NASCAR NEXTEL Cup foe Elliott Sadler during a break in practice.

EA SPORTS 500

OCTOBER 3, 2004
TALLADEGA SUPERSPEEDWAY

Dale Jr.'s crew strides along pit road on the way to join Junior in celebrating the EA Sports 500 win before going to victory lane.

With arms folded, NASCAR NEXTEL Cup championship contenders Dale Earnhardt Jr. and Jeff Gordon strike stern poses before practice. Gordon came into the race riding a two-race winning streak in restrictor-plate races, disrupting the domination of Junior and Dale Earnhardt Inc. teammate Michael Waltrip at Daytona and Talladega.

Dale Jr. smokes his tires as he cuts doughnuts in the infield grass celebrating his win in the EA Sports 500. It was his fifth win in a seven-race span at Talladega Superspeedway.

BANQUET 400

OCTOBER 10, 2004
KANSAS SPEEDWAY

A banner, signed by fans,
wished Junior a Happy 30th
birthday at Kansas Speedway.

Happy 30th, Dale Jr...!!!

KANSAS SPEEDWAY

Dale Jr. leads Jeff Burton through a Kansas Speedway turn number 2.
Junior finished ninth while Burton wound up fifteenth.

Dale Earnhardt Jr. spends time with crew chief Tony Eury Sr. during preparations for the Banquet 400.

UAW-GM
QUALITY 500

OCTOBER 16, 2004
LOWE'S MOTOR SPEEDWAY

A crewman rolls tires away during a four-tire change in the UAW-GM 500. Quick pit stops helped keep Junior in the top five practically the entire distance on the way to a third-place finish

Dale Jr. laps two-time Cup champion Terry Labonte, who announced four days earlier that he will close out his NASCAR NEXTEL Cup Series career by racing 10 times in 2005 and 10 times in 2006.

Dale Jr. laps veteran Ricky Rudd. Junior's car carried a special paint scheme promoting the World Series. The special look was applied after the end of practice the day before. The Budweiser Chevrolet had its normal paint job until then.

SUBWAY 500

OCTOBER 24, 2004

MARTINSVILLE SPEEDWAY

A sell-out crowd filling

Martinsville Speedway

watches Dale Jr. lead

a pack around a newly

repaved turn.

Dale Jr. is followed by Terry Labonte, Jeff Burton and Kevin Harvick as they hook around one of Martinsville's tight turns.

Smoke billows from the front of Dale Jr.'s smashed car after it clipped Kyle Petty's spinning car on lap 476 of the 500-lap race. The crash sidelined Junior, leaving him with a 33rd-place finish and third in points, 125 behind leader Kurt Busch.

BASS PRO SHOPS MBNA 500

OCTOBER 31, 2004

ATLANTA MOTOR SPEEDWAY

Dale Jr. leads Mark Martin into the Atlanta Motor Speedway turn. Dale Jr. wrecked trying to take third place from Carl Edwards with 15 laps to go and missed a golden opportunity to pull even with NASCAR NEXTEL Cup Series standings leader Kurt Busch, who was sidelined by engine failure early. Martin finished second to Jimmie Johnson, after dominating most of the day.

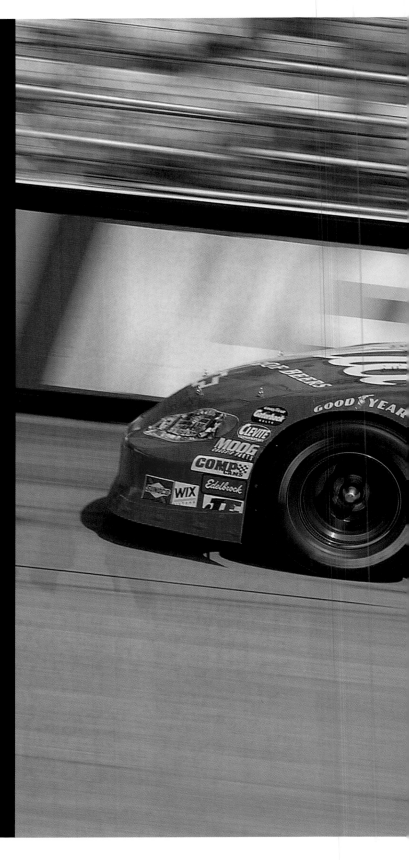

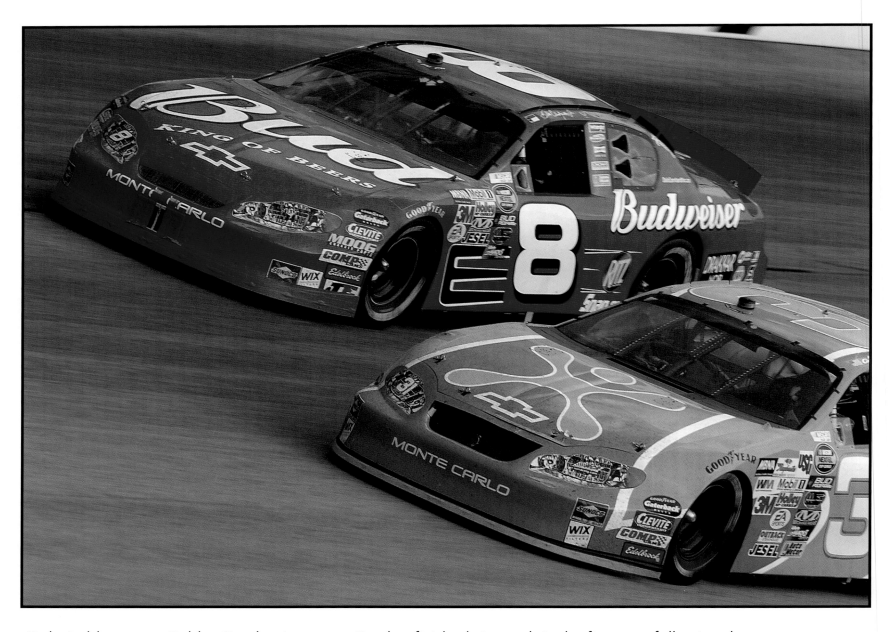

Dale Jr. blows past Robby Gordon in a turn. Gordon finished sixteenth in the first race following the announcement of car owner Richard Childress that Gordon would not return to his Chevrolet next year.

Dale Jr. zips along Atlanta Motor Speedway's front stretch. The 1.54-mile track is one of the fastest tracks on the NASCAR NEXTEL Cup Series with pole qualifying speeds well above 190 miles an hour.

CHECKER AUTO PARTS 500

NOVEMBER 7, 2004

PHOENIX INTERNATIONAL RACEWAY

Dale Jr. leads a pack into a turn on the closing laps of the Checker Auto Parts 500 at Phoenix International Raceway. Junior led 118 laps, including the last 12, in the 315-lap event.

Dale Jr. casually leans against the Budweiser Chevrolet before the start of the Checker Auto Parts 500.

Dale Jr. raises his arms in celebration of his second straight Phoenix International Raceway victory. Junior joined Jeff Burton and Davey Allison as NASCAR Cup Series drivers who have won consecutive races in the annual trips to the "Valley of the Sun."

MOUNTAIN DEW
SOUTHERN 500

NOVEMBER 14, 2004

DARLINGTON RACEWAY

Dale Jr. roars down a straightaway
at historic Darlington Raceway, which
opened in 1950. The straightaways weren't
a problem for Junior, but getting around the
old track's narrow turns were as he battled
a car that was never to his liking.

Dale Jr. and Jeff Green vie for position early in the Southern 500. Dale Jr. escaped disaster when he was able to pit for replacement of a dead battery under a late caution and finished eleventh. Green finished fourteenth.

Dale Jr. tries to stay out of trouble as he skitters through a turn. Earnhardt finished eleventh and left 72 points behind leader Kurt Busch.

FORD 400

NOVEMBER 21, 2004

HOMESTEAD-MIAMI SPEEDWAY

A fish-eye lens provides a panoramic view of Homestead-Miami Speedway's garage area as Dale Jr. backs the Budweiser Chevrolet out of it's stall and heads out to practice. The garage buildings are topped by suites and other viewing areas for spectators.

Dale Jr. receives well wishes from Todd Parrott, the crew chief for Elliott Sadler at Robert Yates Racing. Sadler, one of Earnhardt's best friends among the drivers, was among the 10 qualifiers for the NASCAR NEXTEL Cup Series chase for the championship, but had been mathematically eliminated from having a chance of winning stock-car racing's most coveted crown.

Dale Jr. and members of his team engage in a moment of prayer before he slides into the driver's seat of the Budweiser Chevrolet prior to the start of the Ford 400. Despite a rash of wrecks and a record 14 caution periods, there were no injuries in the final NASCAR Nextel Cup Series race of the season.

THE FANS

Drivers often sign autographs in the garage area as they walk from their cars to their transporter. Here we see fans surrounding Junior as he makes one such trip in the garage area at Daytona International Speedway.

Heading toward his car at Michigan in 2000, Junior stops to sign autographs for fans lined against the pit wall.

Dual-duty. Dale Jr. signs an autograph for a youngster (left) while answering questions from Lee Spencer of the *Sporting News* (right) in 2003 at Martinsville Speedway.

THE PHOTOGRAPHERS

Tom Copeland has been a staff photographer with Cameras In Action Stock Photography for the past two years. He resides in Greensboro, N.C., with his wife Llewellyn and 6-year-old twins Graham and Callie. Before joining CIA, he worked for the News & Record (Greensboro, N.C.) for 12 years. He covered numerous news and sporting events from coastal hurricanes to NCAA Final Fours for the News and Record. In 2002 he was honored with the National Motorsports Press Association's Howard O'Reilly Photographer of the Year Award. He also won the association's Les Lovett Photo of the Year award in 2000 and '02. Copeland served as Photo Editor for "The Petty Family Album: A Tribute to Adam Petty".
When he's not spending time with his family, he enjoys golfing and duck hunting in eastern North Carolina.
Photo courtesy of Harold Hinson

Garry Eller has been employed with Cameras In Action since April 1998. Prior, he received his Bachelors degree in communications from Gardner-Webb University. While at GWU he was a two sport scholarship athlete in wrestling and cross country. During school, a newspaper internship at the Salisbury Post inclined him to think of photography as a career choice. Away from the race track he spends his time fishing and working with local high school wrestling teams.
Garry currently lives in Sherrills Ford, NC.

Ernie Masche from Hickory, NC has been a photographer since 1983. He started covering NASCAR events for the Hickory News in 1983 when Bobby Allison won the Winston Cup Championship. Since that time Ernie has been published by many sources such as UPI, Grand National Scene, Stock Car Racing Magazine, The Sporting News, Sports Illustrated, Autoweek, Car and Driver, UMI Publications, Winston Cup Scene, Winston Cup Illustrated, Fastrack, Speedway Scene, Racing Milestones, Beckett Publications, Reader's Digest, TV Guide and many daily newspapers around the country. Ernie also served as track photographer at Hickory Motor Speedway from 1985 to 1987. In 1989, he was hired as Assistant Photo Editor at Winston Cup Scene. In 1990, he decided to go out on his own and start freelancing as a motorsports photographer. In 1994, Masche and Don Grassmann started Cameras In Action Stock Photography, Inc. Ten years later, CIA Stock Photography, Inc. has become one of the best sources for NASCAR photography in the photo industry. CIA now employs 5 photographers and an office staff to meet the ever demanding needs of some of the biggest corporate sponsors in NASCAR today. Ernie still resides in Hickory with his wife Tamara and son Alex. He likes to spend time with his family, hunting, fishing, scouting and flying RC airplanes.

Andrew Coppley has worked in mortorsports photography for three years. He joined Cameras in Action at the mid point of the 2004 season. He lives in Lexington , N.C. Coppley in a graduate of Randolph Community College in Asheboro, NC.

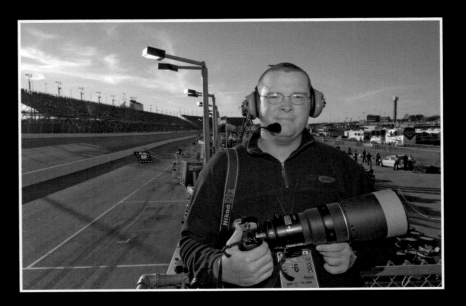

Under a beautiful blue sky on a late fall afternoon in South Florida, Dale Jr. rests against the Budweiser Chevrolet with crewman awaiting the command to climb aboard for the start of the Ford 400. Trailing leader Kurt Busch by 72 points entering the 400-miler and knowing his chance of winning the NASCAR Nextel Cup Series championship was not very good, Junior said his main objective was to have fun. He had very little enjoyment while battling an ill-handling car and being unable to keep pace with the other four championship contenders.